Cupcake
perfection

hinkler

Published by Hinkler Books Pty Ltd
45–55 Fairchild Street
Heatherton Victoria 3202 Australia
www.hinkler.com.au

Text and images © Anthony Carroll 2010
Design © Hinkler Books Pty Ltd 2011

Cover Design: Imagine Graphic Design
Prepress: Graphic Print Group
Typesetting: MPS Limited

ISBN: 978 1 7418 4040 7

Printed and bound in China

Contents

Introduction

The tradition of home baking has always been about putting good food on the table. When the cakes are brought out and the tea or coffee is served, it's an occasion for family, neighbours and friends to take time to sit down and talk, to be with each other and to listen, laugh, remember old times and plan new events. The smell of freshly baked goods and the perfumes of spice wafting through the air will create an environment of gentle anticipation of pleasure and excitement for the young and the young at heart.

Ease and simplicity have always been part of making cupcakes. Once upon a time, back in the early 1800s, they were called 'measure cakes' or 'number cakes' as well as cupcakes because the ingredients were measured by cup, not using a set of scales. It was a quicker way of preparing the recipe during a time when afternoon teas were a way of life. They also derive their name from the fact they were often cooked in a teacup. Teacups, often the second-best ones, would be greased, filled with a simple batter (similar to a pound cake) and baked in a wood- or coal-fired stove. Because the cupcakes were smaller than a normal cake, they required less fuel and less time to cook; perfect for a thrifty housewife!

The recipe for the cupcake has remained a fairly simple affair (although it's rare these days to see someone cooking them in old teacups), however they have evolved to become something slightly more elegant. They're a way for the inventive cook to show off their talents and imagination, from the simple beauty of a plain cupcake with white icing and a glacé (glazed) cherry, to a beautifully decorated little cake with dark chocolate ganache and butter icing flowers. To many people, a batch of cupcakes is a blank canvas on which to paint and decorate, to show their true artistic talents – to others they remain simply… a fast, delicious cake.

Chocolate
indulgence

Double choc cupcakes

2 eggs
125g (4.4oz) butter, softened
1 cup caster (berry) sugar
½ cup milk
2 cups self-raising flour, sifted
100g (3.5oz) dark
(semi-sweet) chocolate pieces
1 tablespoon cocoa powder

Topping

100g (3.5oz) white chocolate,
chopped
20g (0.7oz) butter, softened
⅓ cup thickened
(whipping) cream
1 teaspoon icing sugar
grated dark (semi-sweet)
chocolate to decorate

1   Preheat the oven to 160°C (320°F). Line a 12-cupcake pan with cupcake papers. In a medium-sized bowl, lightly beat the eggs, add butter and sugar, then mix until light and fluffy.

2   Add milk and flour, and stir to combine. Add the dark (semi-sweet) chocolate and cocoa powder, and stir through mixture. Beat with an electric mixer for 2 minutes, until light and creamy.

3   Divide the mixture evenly between the cake papers. Bake for 18–20 minutes until risen and firm to touch. Allow to cool for a few minutes and then transfer to a wire rack. Allow to cool fully before icing.

Topping

1   Meanwhile, combine the white chocolate and butter in a medium-sized saucepan over a medium heat. As the mixture begins to melt, reduce heat to low, stirring constantly, until melted. Remove from heat, add cream and icing sugar, and stir to combine. Rest for 10 minutes: the mixture will be firm and velvety in consistency.

2   Spread icing sugar with the back of a spoon over cupcakes and decorate with grated dark chocolate.

Makes 12 • Preparation 12 minutes • Cooking 20 minutes

Lemon ganache cupcakes

2 eggs
125g (4.4oz) butter, softened
1 cup caster (berry) sugar
½ cup milk
2 cups self-raising flour, sifted
1 teaspoon vanilla extract
100g (3.5oz) dark
(semi-sweet) chocolate pieces
1 tablespoon cocoa powder
1 teaspoon lemon extract

Topping
100g (3.5oz) dark
(semi-sweet) chocolate, grated
20g (0.7oz) butter, softened
⅓ cup thickened
(whipping) cream
1 teaspoon lemon extract
1 piece crystallised (candied)
lemon, cut into slivers

1 Preheat the oven to 160°C (320°F). Line a 12-cupcake pan with cupcake papers. In a medium-sized bowl, lightly beat the eggs, add butter and sugar, then mix until light and fluffy.

2 Add milk, flour and vanilla, and stir to combine. Add remaining ingredients. Beat with an electric mixer for 2 minutes, until light and creamy.

3 Divide the mixture evenly between the cake papers. Bake for 18–20 minutes until risen and firm to touch. Allow to cool for a few minutes and then transfer to a wire rack. Allow to cool fully before icing.

Topping

1 Meanwhile, combine the chocolate and butter in a medium-sized saucepan over a medium heat. As the mixture begins to melt, reduce heat to low, stirring constantly, until melted. Remove from heat, add cream and lemon extract, and stir. Rest for 10 minutes: the mixture will be firm and velvety in consistency.

2 Once cool, put in a piping bag with a small plain nozzle. Pipe topping onto cupcakes in a spiral and top with crystallised (candied) lemon pieces.

Makes 12 • Preparation 12 minutes • Cooking 20 minutes

Chocolate malt cupcakes

2 eggs
125g (4.4oz) butter, softened
1 cup caster (berry) sugar
½ cup buttermilk
2 cups self-raising flour, sifted
1 teaspoon vanilla extract
¼ cup malted milk powder
2 tablespoons cocoa powder

Topping
½ cup chocolate drops
½ cup butter, softened
⅓ cup thickened (whipping) cream
1½ cups icing sugar
1 teaspoon vanilla extract
½ cup chocolate malt balls, crushed

1 Preheat the oven to 160°C (320°F). Line a 12-cupcake pan with cupcake papers. In a medium-sized bowl, lightly beat the eggs, add butter and sugar, then mix until light and fluffy.

2 Add buttermilk, flour, vanilla, malted milk powder and cocoa powder, and stir to combine. Beat with an electric mixer for 2 minutes, until light and creamy.

3 Divide the mixture evenly between the cake papers. Bake for 18–20 minutes until risen and firm to touch. Allow to cool for a few minutes and then transfer to a wire rack. Allow to cool fully before icing.

Topping

1 Meanwhile, combine the chocolate and half of the butter in a medium-sized saucepan over medium heat. As the mixture begins to melt, reduce heat to low, stirring constantly, until melted. Remove from heat, add cream, and stir. Rest for 10 minutes: the mixture will be firm and velvety in consistency.

2 Combine remaining butter, icing sugar and vanilla extract, and stir until light and fluffy. Add melted chocolate mixture, and stir to combine. Apply icing to each cupcake with a knife. Top each cupcake with chocolate malt pieces.

Makes 12 • Preparation 12 minutes • Cooking 20 minutes

Chocolate cupcakes

2 eggs
125g (4.4oz) butter, softened
1 cup caster (berry) sugar
½ cup buttermilk
2 cups self-raising flour, sifted
1 teaspoon cocoa powder
1 teaspoon vanilla extract
½ cup milk chocolate pieces,
finely chopped
⅓ cup unthickened
(half and half/single) cream

Topping
1½ cups icing sugar
½ cup butter, softened
2 tablespoons cocoa powder
sugar (candy) flowers (available
from cake decorating shops)

1   Preheat the oven to 160°C (320°F). Line a 12-cupcake pan with cupcake papers. In a medium-sized bowl, lightly beat the eggs, add butter and sugar, then mix until light and fluffy.
2   Add buttermilk, flour, cocoa powder and vanilla, and stir to combine. Beat with an electric mixer for 2 minutes, until light and creamy. Add chocolate and cream, stir mixture thoroughly.
3   Divide the mixture evenly between the cake papers. Bake for 18–20 minutes until risen and firm to touch. Allow to cool for a few minutes and then transfer to a wire rack. Allow to cool fully before icing.

Topping
1   Meanwhile, combine half the icing sugar and butter, mix with a wooden spoon, add remaining icing sugar, butter and cocoa and beat with the spoon until light and fluffy.
2   Add icing to a piping bag and pipe onto cupcakes, then smooth over with spatula and top with flower decorations.

Makes 12 • Preparation 15 minutes • Cooking 20 minutes

Choc maple cupcakes

2 eggs
125g (4.4oz) butter, softened
1 cup caster (berry) sugar
½ cup milk
1½ cups self-raising flour, sifted
1 teaspoon vanilla extract
100g (3.5oz) dark
(semi-sweet) chocolate pieces
1 tablespoon cocoa powder
½ cup maple syrup

Topping
½ cup butter, softened
2 tablespoons cocoa powder
1½ cups icing sugar
¼ cup maple syrup

1 Preheat the oven to 160°C (320°F). Line a 12-cupcake pan with cupcake papers. In a medium-sized bowl, lightly beat the eggs, add butter and sugar, then mix until light and fluffy.

2 Add milk, flour and vanilla, and stir to combine. Add remaining ingredients. Beat with an electric mixer for 2 minutes, until light and creamy.

3 Divide the mixture evenly between the cake papers. Bake for 18–20 minutes until risen and firm to touch. Allow to cool for a few minutes and then transfer to a wire rack. Allow to cool fully before icing.

Topping
1 Combine topping ingredients, and mix with wooden spoon. Beat with the spoon until light and fluffy. Pipe onto cupcakes using a pipping bag fitted with a small plain nozzle.

Makes 12 • Preparation 12 minutes • Cooking 20 minutes

Choc cherry cupcakes

2 eggs
125g (4.4oz) butter, softened
1 cup caster (berry) sugar
½ cup milk
2 cups self-raising flour, sifted
1 teaspoon vanilla extract
1 tablespoon cocoa powder

Topping

½ cup milk chocolate drops
125g (4.4oz) butter, softened
⅓ cup thickened (whipping) cream
1½ cups icing sugar
1 teaspoon vanilla extract
½ cup glacé (glazed) cherries, chopped
12 whole glacé (glazed) cherries to decorate

1 Preheat the oven to 160°C (320°F). Line a 12-cupcake pan with cupcake papers. In a medium-sized bowl, lightly beat the eggs, add butter and sugar, then mix until light and fluffy.

2 Add milk, flour, vanilla and cocoa powder, and stir to combine. Beat with an electric mixer for 2 minutes, until light and creamy.

3 Divide the mixture evenly between the cake papers. Bake for 18–20 minutes until risen and firm to touch. Allow to cool for a few minutes and then transfer to a wire rack. Allow to cool fully before icing.

Topping

1 Meanwhile, combine the chocolate and half of the butter in a medium-sized saucepan over a medium heat. As the mixture begins to melt, reduce heat to low, stirring constantly, until melted. Remove from heat, add cream, and stir. Rest for 10 minutes: the mixture will be firm and velvety in consistency.

2 Combine remaining butter, icing sugar and vanilla extract, and stir until light and fluffy. Add melted chocolate mixture and stir to combine. Stir through chopped cherries and spread onto cupcakes. Top each with a glacé (glazed) cherry.

Makes 12 • Preparation 20 minutes • Cooking 20 minutes

Dark choc truffle cupcakes

2 eggs
125g (4.4oz) butter, softened
1 cup caster (berry) sugar
½ cup vanilla-flavoured yoghurt
2 cups self-raising flour, sifted
1 tablespoon vanilla extract
100g (3.5oz) dark (semi-sweet) chocolate pieces
1 tablespoon cocoa powder

Topping
100g (3.5oz) dark (semi-sweet) chocolate pieces
20g (0.7oz) butter, softened
⅓ cup thickened (whipping) cream
cocoa powder for dusting

1   Preheat the oven to 160°C (320°F). Line a 12-cupcake pan with cupcake papers. In a medium-sized bowl, lightly beat the eggs, add butter and sugar, then mix until light and fluffy.
2   Add yoghurt, flour and vanilla, and stir to combine. Add remaining ingredients. Beat with an electric mixer for 2 minutes, until light and creamy.
3   Divide the mixture evenly between the cake papers. Bake for 18–20 minutes until risen and firm to touch. Allow to cool for a few minutes, and then transfer to a wire rack. Allow to cool fully before icing.

Topping
1   Meanwhile, combine the chocolate and butter in a medium-sized saucepan over a medium heat. As the mixture begins to melt, reduce heat to low, stirring constantly, until melted. Remove from heat, add cream, and stir. Rest for 10 minutes: the mixture will be firm and velvety in consistency.
2   Use a piping bag fitted with a star nozzle to pipe the mixture onto the cupcakes. Dust heavily with cocoa powder.

Makes 12 • Preparation 12 minutes • Cooking 20 minutes

White choc chip cupcakes

2 eggs
125g (4.4oz) butter, softened
1 cup caster (berry) sugar
½ cup milk
2 cups self-raising flour, sifted
1 teaspoon vanilla extract
½ cup white chocolate drops
1 tablespoon cocoa powder

Topping

½ cup milk chocolate, grated
½ cup butter, softened
⅓ cup thickened (whipping) cream
1½ cups icing sugar
1 teaspoon vanilla extract
½ cup white chocolate drops
½ cup white chocolate drops
to decorate

1   Preheat the oven to 160°C (320°F). Line a 12-cupcake pan with cupcake papers. In a medium-sized bowl, lightly beat the eggs, add butter and sugar, then mix until light and fluffy.

2   Beat with an electric mixer for 2 minutes, until light and creamy. Add milk, flour and vanilla, and stir to combine. Add white chocolate and cocoa powder and stir through mixture.

3   Divide the mixture evenly between the cake papers. Bake for 18–20 minutes until risen and firm to touch. Allow to cool for a few minutes and then transfer to a wire rack. Allow to cool fully before icing.

Topping

1   Meanwhile, combine the milk chocolate and half of the butter in a medium-sized saucepan over a medium heat. As the mixture begins to melt, reduce heat to low, stirring constantly, until melted. Remove from heat, add cream, and stir. Rest for 10 minutes: the mixture will be firm and velvety in consistency.

2   Combine remaining butter, icing sugar and vanilla extract, and stir until light and fluffy. Add melted chocolate mixture, stir in chocolate drops and spoon onto cupcakes. Sprinkle with chocolate drops.

Makes 12 • Preparation 20 minutes • Cooking 20 minutes

White chocolate and sour cream cupcakes

2 eggs
125g (4.4oz) butter, softened
1 cup caster (berry) sugar
½ cup sour cream
2 cups self-raising flour, sifted
1 teaspoon vanilla extract

Topping

100g (3.5oz) white chocolate, coarsely grated
1 tablespoon butter, softened
⅓ cup thickened (whipping) cream
sugar (candy) flowers (available from cake decorating shops)

1 Preheat the oven to 160°C (320°F). Line a 12-cupcake pan with cupcake papers. In a medium-sized bowl, lightly beat the eggs, add butter and sugar, then mix until light and fluffy.
2 Add sour cream, flour and vanilla, and stir to combine. Beat with an electric mixer for 2 minutes, until light and creamy.
3 Divide the mixture evenly between the cake papers. Bake for 18–20 minutes until risen and firm to touch. Allow to cool for a few minutes and then transfer to a wire rack. Allow to cool fully before icing.

Topping

1 Meanwhile, combine the chocolate and butter in a medium-sized saucepan over a medium heat. As the mixture begins to melt, add the cream slowly, then reduce heat to low, stirring constantly, until mixture thickens.
2 Remove from heat and cool. Spread evenly onto cupcakes with a teaspoon, then top with flower decorations.

Makes 12 • Preparation 12 minutes • Cooking 20 minutes

Vanilla and coffee delights

Double vanilla cupcakes

2 eggs
125g (4.4oz) butter, softened
1 cup caster (berry) sugar
½ cup buttermilk
2 cups self-raising flour, sifted
1 teaspoon vanilla extract

Topping
1½ cups icing sugar
125g (4.4oz) butter, softened
seeds scraped from
1 vanilla bean

1   Preheat the oven to 160°C (320°F). Line a 12-cupcake pan with cupcake papers. In a medium-sized bowl, lightly beat the eggs, add butter and sugar, then mix until light and fluffy.
2   Add buttermilk, flour and vanilla, and stir to combine. Beat with an electric mixer for 2 minutes, until light and creamy.
3   Divide the mixture evenly between the cake papers. Bake for 18–20 minutes until risen and firm to touch. Allow to cool for a few minutes and then transfer to a wire rack. Allow to cool fully before icing.

Topping
1   Meanwhile, combine half the topping ingredients except vanilla bean seeds and stir with a wooden spoon until mixed together. Add remaining ingredients and beat with the spoon until light and fluffy.
2   Spoon topping onto cakes using the back of a spoon.

Makes 12 • Preparation 12 minutes • Cooking 20 minutes

Persian vanilla saffron cupcakes

2 eggs
125g (4.4oz) butter, softened
1 cup caster (berry) sugar
½ cup milk
2 cups self-raising flour, sifted
1 teaspoon vanilla extract
1 pinch saffron strands

Topping
1½ cups icing sugar
1 teaspoon lemon extract
1 teaspoon vanilla extract
125g (4.4oz) butter, softened
Persian fairy (candy) floss

1   Preheat the oven to 160°C (320°F). Line a 12-cupcake pan with cupcake papers. In a medium-sized bowl, lightly beat the eggs, add butter and sugar, then mix until light and fluffy.
2   Add milk, flour, vanilla and saffron, and stir to combine. Beat with an electric mixer for 2 minutes, until light and creamy.
3   Divide the mixture evenly between the cake papers. Bake for 18–20 minutes until risen and firm to touch. Allow to cool for a few minutes and then transfer to a wire rack. Allow to cool fully before icing.

Topping
1   Meanwhile, combine all topping ingredients except fairy (candy) floss, mix with a wooden spoon until well combined, and beat with the spoon until light and fluffy.
2   Place mixture into a piping bag with a star-shaped nozzle and pipe onto all cupcakes. Top with fairy floss.

Makes 12 • Preparation 12 minutes • Cooking 20 minutes

Melting marshmallow cupcakes

2 eggs
125g (4.4oz) butter, softened
1 cup caster (berry) sugar
½ cup buttermilk
2 cups self-raising flour, sifted
2 teaspoons vanilla extract
100g (3.5oz) mini marshmallows

Topping
1½ cups icing sugar
125g (4.4oz) butter, softened
1 teaspoon vanilla extract
100g (3.5oz) mini
marshmallows, melted
pink and white sprinkles
to decorate

1 Preheat the oven to 160°C (320°F). Line a 12-cupcake pan with cupcake papers. In a medium-sized bowl, lightly beat the eggs, add butter and sugar, then mix until light and fluffy.

2 Add buttermilk, flour and vanilla, and stir to combine. Beat with an electric mixer for 2 minutes, until light and creamy, then stir through marshmallows.

3 Divide the mixture evenly between the cake papers. Bake for 18–20 minutes until risen and firm to touch. Allow to cool for a few minutes and then transfer to a wire rack. Allow to cool fully before icing.

Topping

1 Meanwhile, combine half the icing sugar and butter and mix with a wooden spoon. Add remaining icing sugar, butter and vanilla extract and beat with the spoon until light and fluffy. Stir in melted marshmellows.

2 Spoon topping onto each cupcake using the back of a spoon and top with sprinkles.

To melt marshmallows, microwave them on high for 20 seconds at a time until melted

Makes 12 • Preparation 12 minutes • Cooking 20 minutes

Vanilla snowflake cupcakes

2 eggs
125g (4.4oz) butter, softened
1 cup caster (berry) sugar
½ cup milk
2 cups self-raising flour, sifted
1 teaspoon vanilla extract

Topping
1½ cups icing sugar
125g (4.4oz) butter, softened
white sprinkles to decorate

1 Preheat the oven to 160°C (320°F). Line a 12-cupcake pan with cupcake papers. In a medium-sized bowl, lightly beat the eggs, add butter and sugar, then mix until light and fluffy.

2 Add milk, flour and vanilla, and stir to combine. Beat with an electric mixer for 2 minutes, until light and creamy.

3 Divide the mixture evenly between the cake papers. Bake for 18–20 minutes until risen and firm to touch. Allow to cool for a few minutes and then transfer to a wire rack. Allow to cool fully before icing.

Topping

1 Meanwhile, combine half the icing sugar and butter, mix with a wooden spoon, add the remaining icing sugar and butter and beat with the spoon until light and fluffy.

2 Use a piping bag fitted with a round nozzle to pipe the topping onto the cupcakes. Top with white sprinkles.

Makes 12 • Preparation 12 minutes • Cooking 20 minutes

Vanilla valentine cupcakes

2 eggs
125g (4.4oz) butter, softened
1 cup caster (berry) sugar
½ cup milk
2 cups self-raising flour, sifted
1 teaspoon vanilla extract
100g (3.5oz) white chocolate, chopped

Topping
1 cup icing sugar
2 tablespoons water
few drops pink colouring
tube of white or silver icing

1. Preheat the oven to 160°C (320°F). Line a 12-cupcake pan with cupcake papers. In a medium-sized bowl, lightly beat the eggs, add butter and sugar, then mix until light and fluffy.

2. Add milk, flour and vanilla, and stir to combine. Beat with an electric mixer for 2 minutes, until light and creamy. Add white chocolate and stir through the mixture.

3. Divide the mixture evenly between the cake papers. Bake for 18–20 minutes until risen and firm to touch. Allow to cool for a few minutes and then transfer to a wire rack. Allow to cool fully before icing.

Topping

1. Meanwhile, combine icing sugar and water in a small bowl and mix to make a smooth paste, adding more water if necessary. Tint with pink colouring.

2. Spread evenly over each cupcake. Pipe hearts onto each cupcake with tube icing.

Makes 12 • Preparation 12 minutes • Cooking 20 minutes

Morning coffee cupcakes

2 cups self-raising flour
4½ tablespoons instant coffee
125g (4.4oz) butter, softened
¼ teaspoon vanilla extract
1 cup caster (berry) sugar
2 eggs
¼ cup milk
¼ cup Amaretto

Topping
1½ cups icing sugar
½ cup milk powder
100g (3.5oz) butter, softened
2 tablespoons milk
4 drops vanilla extract
1 tablespoon instant coffee

1   Preheat the oven to 180°C (350°F). Line a 12-cupcake pan with cupcake papers. Sift the dry ingredients together.
2   In a medium-sized bowl, beat the butter, vanilla and sugar with an electric mixer until creamy. Add the eggs one at a time and beat until well combined.
3   Add the dry ingredients, milk and Amaretto to the butter mixture and combine thoroughly.
4   Divide the mixture evenly between the cake papers. Bake for approximately 20 minutes until risen and firm to touch. Allow to cool for a few minutes and then transfer to a wire rack. Allow to cool fully before icing.

Topping
1   Meanwhile, combine all of the ingredients except the instant coffee in a medium-sized bowl and beat with an electric mixer on slow for 1 minute. Turn speed up and beat until light and fluffy. Add 1 teaspoon of water to the coffee and add to the topping, stirring only once.
2   Spread topping evenly onto cupcakes with the back of a teaspoon.

Makes 12 • Preparation 20 minutes • Cooking 20 minutes

21

Mocha choc chip cupcakes

2 eggs
125g (4.4oz) butter, softened
1 cup caster (berry) sugar
½ cup milk
1 teaspoon vanilla extract
2 cups self-raising flour, sifted
2 tablespoons instant coffee
½ cup mini chocolate chips

Topping
1½ cups icing sugar
125g (4.4oz) butter, softened
1 teaspoon instant coffee
mini chocolate chips to decorate

1   Preheat the oven to 160°C (320°F). Line a 12-cupcake pan with cupcake papers. In a medium sized bowl, lightly beat the eggs, add butter and sugar, then mix until light and fluffy.
2   Add milk, vanilla, flour and coffee, and stir to combine. Beat with an electric mixer for 2 minutes until light and fluffy. Stir through the chocolate chips.
3   Divide the mixture between the cake papers. Bake for 18–20 minutes until risen and firm to the touch. Allow to cool for a few minutes, then transfer to a wire rack. Allow to cool fully before icing.

Topping
1   Mix together the icing sugar, butter and coffee until well combined, then beat until light and fluffy.
2   Use a piping bag fitted with a star nozzle to pipe the topping onto the cupcakes. Decorate with chocolate chips.

Makes 12 • Preparation 12 minutes • Cooking 20 minutes

Coffee walnut cupcakes

2 cups self-raising flour, sifted
¼ cup chopped walnuts
125g (4.4oz) butter, softened
1 cup caster (berry) sugar
2 teaspoons instant coffee
2 eggs
½ cup milk

Topping

1 cup icing sugar
1 teaspoon instant coffee
2–3 tablespoons boiling water
12 whole walnut halves

1 Preheat the oven to 200°C (400°F). Line a 12-cupcake pan with cupcake papers.

2 Combine the flour and walnuts in a medium-sized bowl. Beat the butter, sugar and coffee in a large bowl until creamy. Add the eggs, one at a time, until just blended. Fold in the dry ingredients and milk.

3 Divide the mixture evenly between the cake papers. Bake for 12–15 minutes until risen and firm to touch. Allow to cool for a few minutes and then transfer to a wire rack. Allow to cool fully before icing.

Topping

1 Combine the icing sugar and coffee, and mix with enough water to make a soft icing.

2 Apply icing to each cupcake with a knife and top each cupcake with a walnut half.

Makes 12 • Preparation 10 minutes • Cooking 15 minutes

French coffee cupcakes

125g (4.4oz) butter, softened
¼ cup milk
2 tablespoons milk powder
1 tablespoon instant coffee
2 eggs
1 cup caster (berry) sugar
2 cups self-raising flour, sifted
½ cup Grand Marnier

Topping
1½ cups icing sugar
¼ cup milk powder
125g (4.4oz) butter, softened
1 tablespoon Grand Marnier
crystallised (candied) orange
zest to decorate

1   Preheat the oven to 180°C (350°F). Line a 12-cupcake pan with cupcake papers. In a saucepan, heat the butter, milk, milk powder and coffee gently and stir until butter is melted. Allow to cool.

2   In a large bowl, whisk the eggs with an electric mixer until thick and creamy. Add the sugar gradually, then stir in half the butter mixture and flour and beat. Add the Grand Marnier, then the remaining butter mixture and flour and beat until smooth.

3   Divide the mixture evenly between the cake papers. Bake for 20 minutes until risen and firm to touch. Allow to cool for a few minutes and then transfer to a wire rack. Allow to cool fully before icing.

Topping

1   Meanwhile, combine all of the ingredients except the Grand Marnier and orange zest in a medium-sized bowl and beat with an electric mixer for 1 minute. Turn speed up and beat until light and fluffy. Add the Grand Marnier slowly and mix again until thoroughly combined.

2   Place mixture into a piping bag and pipe onto all cupcakes. Sprinkle with the orange zest.

Makes 12 • Preparation 20 minutes • Cooking 20 minutes

Italian coffee cupcakes

125g (4.4oz) butter, softened
½ cup milk, scalded then cooled
½ teaspoon vanilla extract
2 eggs
1 cup caster (berry) sugar
2 cups self-raising flour, sifted
1½ tablespoons skim milk powder
1 tablespoon instant coffee
2 tablespoons Amaretto

Topping

1½ cups icing sugar
½ cup milk powder
1 tablespoon instant coffee
100g (3.5oz) butter, softened
2 tablespoons milk
4 drops vanilla extract
2 tablespoons Amaretto
cocoa powder to dust

1 Preheat the oven to 180°C (350°F). Line a 12-cupcake pan with cupcake papers. In a saucepan, heat the butter, ¼ cup of milk and vanilla gently and stir until butter is melted. Add the remaining milk and allow to cool.

2 In a large bowl, whisk the eggs with an electric mixer until thick and creamy. Add the sugar gradually, then stir in half the butter mixture and half of the flour and beat. Add the remaining butter mixture, flour, skim milk powder, coffee and Amaretto and beat until smooth.

3 Divide the mixture evenly between the cake papers. Bake for 20 minutes until risen and firm to touch. Allow to cool for a few minutes and then transfer to a wire rack. Allow to cool fully before icing.

Topping

1 Meanwhile, combine all of the ingredients except the cocoa powder in a medium-sized bowl and beat with an electric mixer on slow for 1 minute. Turn speed up and beat for 5 minutes until light and fluffy.

2 Place mixture into a piping bag, pipe onto all cupcakes and dust with cocoa powder.

Makes 12 • Preparation 20 minutes • Cooking 20 minutes

Mexican coffee cupcakes

2 cups self-raising flour
2 tablespoons cocoa powder
2 tablespoons instant coffee
125g (4.4oz) butter, softened
½ teaspoon vanilla extract
1 cup caster (berry) sugar
2 eggs
¼ cup milk
¼ cup Kahlua

Topping
1 tablespoon instant coffee
200mL thickened (whipped) cream
2 tablespoons Kahlua
250g (9oz) dark chocolate, finely chopped

1 Preheat the oven to 180°C (350°F). Line a 12-cupcake pan with cupcake papers. Sift the dry ingredients together.
2 In a medium-sized bowl, beat the butter, vanilla and sugar with an electric mixer until creamy. Add the eggs one at a time and beat until well combined.
3 Add the dry ingredients to the butter mixture and combine thoroughly, then slowly add the milk and Kahlua and mix again.
4 Divide the mixture evenly between the cake papers. Bake for approximately 20 minutes until risen and firm to touch. Allow to cool for a few minutes and then transfer to a wire rack. Allow to cool fully before icing.

Topping
1 Meanwhile, heat the coffee, cream and Kahlua gently in a saucepan. Place chopped chocolate into a medium-sized bowl. Pour mixture over the chocolate to melt it, and stir thoroughly.
2 Place mixture into a piping bag with a star-shaped nozzle and pipe onto all cupcakes.

Makes 12 • Preparation 12 minutes • Cooking 20 minutes

Fruity and nutty treats

Raspberry cupcakes

2 eggs
125g (4.4oz) butter, softened
1 cup caster (berry) sugar
½ cup milk
2 cups self-raising flour, sifted
1 teaspoon vanilla extract
¼ cup raspberries, crushed

Topping
1½ cups icing sugar
125g (4.4oz) butter, softened
sugared raspberries

1 Preheat the oven to 160°C (320°F). Line a 12-cupcake pan with cupcake papers. In a medium-sized bowl, lightly beat the eggs, add butter and sugar, then mix until light and fluffy.
2 Add milk, flour and vanilla, and stir to combine. Beat with an electric mixer for 2 minutes, until light and creamy. Stir in crushed raspberries.
3 Divide the mixture evenly between the cake papers. Bake for 18–20 minutes until risen and firm to touch. Allow to cool for a few minutes and then transfer to a wire rack. Allow to cool fully before icing.

Topping
1 Meanwhile, combine icing sugar and butter in a small bowl, mix with a wooden spoon until well combined, then beat with a whisk until light and fluffy.
2 Spoon mixture into a piping bag with a medium-sized star-shaped nozzle. Pipe icing onto each cupcake and decorate with the sugared raspberries. Serve immediately.

To sugar the raspberries, brush with lightly beaten pasteurised egg whites and dust with caster (berry) sugar

Makes 12 • Preparation 12 minutes • Cooking 20 minutes

Raspberry coconut cupcakes

2 eggs
125g (4.4oz) butter, softened
1 cup caster (berry) sugar
½ cup milk
2 tablespoons raspberry liqueur
¼ cup dessicated (fine) coconut
2 cups self-raising flour, sifted

Topping
1 cup icing sugar
2 tablespoons water
1 punnet (125g/4.4oz) raspberries
coconut flakes

1 Preheat the oven to 160°C (320°F). Line a 12-cupcake pan with cupcake papers. In a medium-sized bowl, lightly beat the eggs, add butter and sugar, then mix until light and fluffy.

2 Add milk, liqueur, coconut and flour, and stir to combine. Beat with an electric mixer for 2 minutes, until light and creamy.

3 Divide the mixture evenly between the cake papers. Bake for 18–20 minutes until risen and firm to touch. Allow to cool for a few minutes and then transfer to a wire rack. Allow to cool fully before icing.

Topping
1 Meanwhile, combine icing sugar and water in a small bowl. Spread icing over each cupcake. Decorate with raspberries and shaved coconut.

Makes 12 • Preparation 12 minutes • Cooking 20 minutes

Cherry sour cream butter cupcakes

125g (4.4oz) butter, softened
1 teaspoon vanilla extract
zest of 1 large lemon
1 cup caster (berry) sugar
2 eggs
2 cups self-raising flour, sifted
⅓ cup sour cream
¼ cup chopped morello cherries

Topping

1½ cups icing sugar
zest of 1 lemon
½ teaspoon lemon juice
125g (4.4oz) butter, softened
morello cherries to decorate

1   Preheat the oven to 160°C (320°F). Line a 12-cupcake pan with cupcake papers. In a bowl, beat the butter, vanilla, lemon zest and sugar with an electric mixer until light and fluffy.

2   Beat in the eggs one at a time, scraping down the bowl between additions. Stir in half the flour and sour cream. Blend well. Mix in the remaining flour and sour cream, and mix thoroughly but gently. Stir in cherries.

3   Divide the mixture evenly between the cake papers. Bake for 18–20 minutes until risen and firm to touch. Allow to cool for a few minutes and then transfer to a wire rack. Allow to cool fully before icing.

Topping

1   Meanwhile, combine all ingredients except cherries and beat with an electric mixer for 5 minutes until creamy. Spoon mixture into a piping bag and decorate the top of each cake in a spiral. Top with cherries.

Makes 12 • Preparation 15 minutes • Cooking 20 minutes

Pear and cinnamon cupcakes

½ pear, peeled and chopped into small pieces
juice of 1 lemon
1 tablespoon cinnamon
2 eggs
125g (4.4oz) butter, softened
1 cup caster (berry) sugar
½ cup milk
2 cups self-raising flour, sifted

Topping
1½ cups icing sugar
125g (4.4oz) butter, softened
1 tablespoon cinnamon sugar

1   Preheat the oven to 160°C (320°F). Line a 12-cupcake pan with cupcake papers. In a small bowl, coat the pear pieces with lemon juice and sprinkle with cinnamon. In a medium-sized bowl, lightly beat the eggs, add butter and sugar, then mix until light and fluffy.

2   Add milk and flour, and stir to combine. Beat with an electric mixer for 2 minutes, until light and creamy. Add spiced pear and stir through mixture.

3   Divide the mixture evenly between the cake papers. Bake for 18–20 minutes until risen and firm to touch. Allow to cool for a few minutes and then transfer to a wire rack. Allow to cool fully before icing.

Topping

1   Meanwhile, combine half the icing sugar and butter, mix with a wooden spoon, add remaining icing sugar and butter and beat with the spoon until light and fluffy. Spoon mixture into piping bag and decorate the top of each cake in a spiral. Sprinkle cinnamon sugar on top.

Makes 12 • Preparation 12 minutes • Cooking 20 minutes

Sugar plum cupcakes

2 eggs
125g (4.4oz) butter, softened
1 cup caster (berry) sugar
½ cup milk
2 cups self-raising flour, sifted
2 tablespoons plum liqueur
¼ cup chopped plums

Topping

1½ cups icing sugar
125g (4.4oz) butter, softened
1 drop purple food colouring
sugar (candy) flowers
(available from
cake decorating shops)

1   Preheat the oven to 160°C (320°F). Line a
    12-cupcake pan with cupcake papers. In a
    medium-sized bowl, lightly beat the eggs, add
    butter and sugar, then mix until light and fluffy.

2   Add milk, flour and plum liqueur, and stir
    to combine. Beat with an electric mixer for
    5 minutes, until light and creamy, then stir in
    chopped plums.

3   Divide the mixture evenly between the cake
    papers. Bake for 18–20 minutes. Allow to cool
    for a few minutes and then transfer to a wire
    rack. Allow to cool fully before icing.

Topping

1   Combine all ingredients except sugar (candy)
    flowers in a small bowl, mix with a wooden
    spoon, then whisk until light and fluffy. Place
    mixture into a piping bag and pipe onto all
    cupcakes. Decorate with sugar flowers.

Makes 12 • Preparation 12 minutes • Cooking 20 minutes

Double berry cupcakes

2 eggs

125g (4.4oz) butter, softened

1 cup caster (berry) sugar

½ cup milk

2 cups self-raising flour, sifted

1 teaspoon vanilla extract

¼ punnet (30g) blueberries, chopped in half

¼ punnet (60g) strawberries, chopped

Topping

2 cups icing sugar

2 tablespoons of blueberries, mashed

2 tablespoons strawberries, mashed

½ punnet (60 g) blueberries

¼ punnet (60g) strawberries, quartered

1 Preheat the oven to 160°C (320°F). Line a 12-cupcake pan with cupcake papers. In a medium-sized bowl, lightly beat the eggs, add butter and sugar, then mix until light and fluffy.

2 Add milk, flour and vanilla, and stir to combine. Beat with an electric mixer for 2 minutes, until light and creamy. Add blueberries and strawberries and stir through the mixture.

3 Divide the mixture evenly between the cake papers. Bake for 18–20 minutes until risen and firm to touch. Allow to cool for a few minutes and then transfer to a wire rack. Allow to cool fully before icing.

Topping

1 Meanwhile, combine icing sugar and mashed berries in a medium-sized bowl and mix with a wooden spoon. Use a spatula to apply icing to each cupcake and top with a blueberry and strawberry quarters.

Makes 12 • Preparation 12 minutes • Cooking 20 minutes

Apple nut cupcakes

2 eggs
125g (4.4oz) butter, softened
1 cup caster (berry) sugar
½ cup milk
2 cups self-raising flour, sifted
¼ cup smooth peanut butter
1 small green apple, grated

Topping

½ cup caster (berry) sugar,
for toffee
1½ cups icing sugar
125g (4.4oz) butter, softened
2 tablespoons crunchy
unsalted peanut butter

1 Preheat the oven to 160°C (320°F). Line a 12-cupcake pan with cupcake papers. In a medium-sized bowl, lightly beat the eggs, add butter and sugar, then mix until light and fluffy.
2 Add milk, flour and peanut butter, and stir to combine. Beat with an electric mixer for 2 minutes, until light and creamy. Add apple and stir through mix.
3 Divide the mixture evenly between the cake papers. Bake for 18–20 minutes until risen and firm to touch. Allow to cool for a few minutes and then transfer to a wire rack. Allow to cool fully before icing.

Toffee

1 Place caster (berry) sugar evenly on a greaseproof paper–lined baking tray, and bake at 200°C for approximately 25 minutes until toffee consistency forms. Cool until hardened.

Topping

1 Meanwhile, combine half the icing sugar, butter and peanut butter, and mix with a wooden spoon. Add remaining icing sugar, butter and peanut butter and beat with the spoon until light and fluffy.
2 Use the back of a spoon to ice cakes. Top with broken toffee pieces.

Makes 12 • Preparation 12 minutes • Cooking 45 minutes

White chocolate and pistachio cupcakes

2 eggs
125g (4.4oz) butter, softened
1 cup caster (berry) sugar
½ cup milk
2 cups self-raising flour, sifted
1 teaspoon vanilla extract
zest and juice of ½ lemon
½ cup pistachios
½ cup white chocolate chips

Topping

1½ cups icing sugar
125g (4.4oz) butter, softened
juice of ½ lemon
½ cup pistachios
grated white chocolate to decorate

1 Preheat the oven to 160°C (320°F). Line a 12-cupcake pan with cupcake papers. In a medium-sized bowl, lightly beat the eggs, add butter and sugar, then mix until light and fluffy.

2 Add milk, flour, vanilla, lemon zest and juice, and stir to combine. Beat with an electric mixer for 2 minutes, until light and creamy. Add pistachios and white chocolate and combine.

3 Divide the mixture evenly between the cake papers. Bake for 18–20 minutes until risen and firm to touch. Allow to cool for a few minutes and then transfer to a wire rack. Allow to cool fully before icing.

Topping

1 Meanwhile, combine icing sugar, butter and lemon juice, mix with a wooden spoon until well combined, and beat with the spoon until light and fluffy. Add pistachios and mix through. Spoon onto cupcakes in large, loose dollops. Sprinkle with grated chocolate.

Makes 12 • Preparation 12 minutes • Cooking 20 minutes

Macadamia choc cupcakes

3 eggs
125g (4.4oz) butter, softened
1 cup caster (berry) sugar
½ cup milk
1½ cups self-raising flour, sifted
1 teaspoon vanilla extract
1 tablespoon cocoa powder
¼ cup chopped macadamias

Topping

½ cup caster (berry) sugar,
for toffee
100g (3.5oz) dark (semi-sweet)
chocolate
20g (0.7oz) butter, softened
⅓ cup thickened (whipping) cream
1 cup icing sugar
1 tablespoon cocoa powder
100g chopped macadamias

1 Preheat the oven to 160°C (320°F). Line a 12-cupcake pan with cupcake papers. In a medium-sized bowl, lightly beat the eggs, add butter and sugar, then mix until light and fluffy.

2 Add milk, flour, vanilla and cocoa powder, and stir to combine. Beat with an electric mixer for 2 minutes, until light and creamy, then stir in macadamias.

3 Divide the mixture evenly between the cake papers. Bake for 18–20 minutes until risen and firm to touch. Allow to cool for a few minutes and then transfer to a wire rack. Allow to cool fully before icing.

Toffee

1 Place caster (berry) sugar evenly on a greaseproof paper–lined baking tray, and bake at 200°C for approximately 25 minutes until toffee consistency forms. Cool until hardened.

Topping

1 Combine the chocolate and butter in a medium-sized saucepan over a medium heat. As the mixture begins to melt, reduce heat to low, stirring constantly, until melted. Remove from heat, add cream, and stir. Rest for 10 minutes: the mixture will be firm and velvety in consistency.

2 Combine the icing sugar and cocoa powder. Add the chocolate mixture and mix with a wooden spoon until light and fluffy. Spread evenly onto the cupcakes with a teaspoon or spatula. Decorate with macadamia and broken toffee pieces.

Makes 12 • Preparation 12 minutes • Cooking 45 minutes

Citrus
flavours

Lemon poppy cupcakes

2 eggs
125g (4.4oz) butter, softened
1 cup caster (berry) sugar
½ cup Greek-style yoghurt
2 cups self-raising flour, sifted
zest of 2 lemons
juice of 1 lemon
1 teaspoon poppy seeds

Topping
1½ cups icing sugar
125g (4.4oz) butter, softened
juice of 1 lemon
½ teaspoon poppy seeds
zest of 1 lemon
50g (1.8oz) crystallised (candied)
lemon, cut into thin slivers

1 Preheat the oven to 160°C (320°F). Line a 12-cupcake pan with cupcake papers. In a medium-sized bowl, lightly beat the eggs, add butter and sugar, then mix until light and fluffy.
2 Add yoghurt and flour, and stir to combine. Beat with an electric mixer for 2 minutes, until light and creamy. Stir through lemon zest, lemon juice and poppy seeds.
3 Divide the mixture evenly between the cake papers. Bake for 18–20 minutes until risen and firm to touch. Allow to cool for a few minutes and then transfer to a wire rack. Allow to cool fully before icing.

Topping
1 Meanwhile, combine all the topping ingredients except the crystallised (candied) lemon, mix and spoon onto cakes. Top with crystallised lemon pieces.

Makes 12 • Preparation 12 minutes • Cooking 20 minutes

Lemon passion cupcakes

2 eggs
125g (4.4oz) butter, softened
1 cup caster (berry) sugar
½ cup plain yoghurt
2 cups self-raising flour, sifted
1 teaspoon vanilla extract
pulp of 2 passionfruit
1 teaspoon lemon zest

Topping
1 cup lemon butter
pulp of 1 passionfruit

1. Preheat the oven to 160°C (320°F). Line a 12-cupcake pan with cupcake papers. In a medium-sized bowl, lightly beat the eggs, add butter and sugar, then mix until light and fluffy.

2. Add yoghurt, flour and vanilla, and stir to combine. Beat with an electric mixer for 2 minutes, until light and creamy. Fold passionfruit pulp and lemon zest through mixture.

3. Divide the mixture evenly between the cake papers. Bake for 18–20 minutes until risen and firm to touch. Allow to cool for a few minutes and then transfer to a wire rack. Allow to cool fully before icing.

Topping
1. Meanwhile, combine lemon butter and passionfruit in a medium-sized bowl and mix with a wooden spoon. Spread topping on cupcakes.

Makes 12 • Preparation 12 minutes • Cooking 20 minutes

Ginger zinger cupcakes

2 eggs
125g (4.4oz) butter, softened
1 cup caster (berry) sugar
½ cup buttermilk
2 cups self-raising flour, sifted
½ cup crystallised (candied) ginger, finely chopped
juice of ½ lemon
zest of 1 lemon

Topping
1 cup icing sugar
2 tablespoons lemon juice
50g (1.7oz) glacé (glazed) ginger

1 Preheat the oven to 160°C (320°F). Line a 12-cupcake pan with cupcake papers. In a medium-sized bowl, lightly beat the eggs, add butter and sugar, then mix until light and fluffy.

2 Add buttermilk and flour, and stir to combine. Beat with an electric mixer for 2 minutes, until light and creamy. Add crystallised (candied) ginger, lemon juice and zest, and mix thoroughly.

3 Divide the mixture evenly between the cake papers. Bake for 18–20 minutes until risen and firm to touch. Allow to cool for a few minutes and then transfer to a wire rack. Allow to cool fully before icing.

Topping
1 Mix icing sugar with enough lemon juice to make a smooth paste. Spread evenly over the cupcakes. Top with slices of glacé (glazed) ginger.

Makes 12 • Preparation 12 minutes • Cooking 20 minutes

Blood orange poppy cupcakes

2 eggs
125g (4.4oz) butter, softened
1 cup caster (berry) sugar
½ cup buttermilk
2 cups self-raising flour, sifted
zest of 1 blood orange
juice of ½ blood orange
1 teaspoon poppy seeds

Topping

1½ cups icing sugar
125g (4.4oz) butter, softened
zest of 1 blood orange
juice of ½ blood orange
½ teaspoon poppy seeds
crystallised (candied) orange
pieces, cut into thin slivers

1 Preheat the oven to 160°C (320°F). Line a 12-cupcake pan with cupcake papers. In a medium-sized bowl, lightly beat the eggs, add butter and sugar, then mix until light and fluffy.

2 Add buttermilk and flour, and stir to combine. Beat with an electric mixer for 2 minutes, until light and creamy. Add orange zest, orange juice and poppy seeds, and mix through with a wooden spoon.

3 Divide the mixture evenly between the cake papers. Bake for 18–20 minutes until risen and firm to touch. Allow to cool for a few minutes and then transfer to a wire rack. Allow to cool fully before icing.

Topping

1 Meanwhile, combine topping ingredients except crystallised (candied) orange, and mix with a wooden spoon. Spoon onto cakes. Top with crystallised orange pieces.

Makes 12 • Preparation 12 minutes • Cooking 20 minutes

41

Choc orange cupcakes

2 eggs
125g (4.4oz) butter, softened
1 cup caster (berry) sugar
½ cup milk
2 cups self-raising flour, sifted
1 teaspoon cocoa powder
1 teaspoon vanilla extract
juice of 1 orange
zest of 1 orange
¼ cup chocolate chips or flakes

Topping
2 cups icing sugar
125g (4.4oz) butter, softened
¼ cup orange juice
crushed chocolate orange balls
to decorate

1 Preheat the oven to 160°C (320°F). Line a 12-cupcake pan with cupcake papers. In a medium-sized bowl, lightly beat the eggs, add butter and sugar, then mix until light and fluffy.
2 Add milk, flour, cocoa powder and vanilla, and stir to combine. Beat with an electric mixer for 2 minutes, until light and creamy. Add juice, zest and chocolate chips and stir to combine.
3 Divide the mixture evenly between the cake papers. Bake for 18–20 minutes until risen and firm to touch. Allow to cool for a few minutes and then transfer to a wire rack. Allow to cool fully before icing.

Topping
1 Meanwhile, combine half of all the topping ingredients except chocolate balls, mix with a wooden spoon, add remaining ingredients except chocolate balls and beat with the spoon until light and fluffy. Use a piping bag fitted with a star nozzle to pipe the icing onto the cupcakes. Top with chocolate ball pieces.

Makes 12 • Preparation 12 minutes • Cooking 20 minutes

Lemon and lime cupcakes

2 cups self-raising flour, sifted

1 cup caster (berry) sugar

125g (4.4oz) butter, softened

2 eggs

½ cup buttermilk

1 teaspoon lemon extract

1 teaspoon lime extract

zest of 1 lime

zest of 1 lemon

Sugared citrus zest

zest of 3 limes

zest of 3 lemons

¾ cup caster (berry) sugar

Topping

125g (4.4oz) unsalted butter, softened

½ teaspoon lime extract

½ teaspoon lemon extract

1½ cups icing sugar

1. Preheat the oven to 180°C (350°F). Line a 12-cupcake pan with cupcake papers. Place all the ingredients except the zest in a bowl, and beat with an electric mixer for 5 minutes until pale and fluffy. Fold in the zest.

2. Divide the mixture evenly between the cake papers. Bake for 20–25 minutes until risen and firm to touch. Allow to cool for a few minutes and then transfer to a wire rack. Allow to cool fully before icing.

Sugared citrus zest

1. Meanwhile, to make the sugared citrus zest, coat the lime and lemon zest with caster (berry) sugar and toss to thoroughly combine. Leave for at least 10 minutes.

Topping

1. Beat the butter with an electric mixer for 2 minutes and add extracts and half of the icing sugar. Beat for 3 minutes. Add the rest of the sugar and beat for a further 3 minutes.

2. Add mixture to piping bag, pipe onto cakes and top with the sugared citrus zest.

Makes 12 • Preparation 35 minutes • Cooking 25 minutes

Citrus burst cupcakes

2 eggs
1 cup caster (berry) sugar
½ cup vegetable oil
¼ cup lemon juice
zest of 1 lemon
zest of 1 lime
2 cups plain flour
2 teaspoons baking powder
½ cup almond meal

Topping
1½ cups icing sugar
zest of 1 lemon
1 teaspoon lemon juice
90g (3.2oz) butter, softened
crystallised (candied) lime, lemon
and orange zest
to decorate

1 Preheat the oven to 180°C (350°F). Line a 12-cupcake pan with cupcake papers. In a medium-sized bowl, beat eggs, sugar, oil, lemon juice and zest with an electric mixer until thoroughly combined and creamy.

2 Sift the flour and baking powder into a bowl, then add the almond meal and lemon and egg mixture, and beat for 5 minutes.

3 Divide the mixture evenly between the cake papers. Bake for 20–25 minutes. Allow to cool for a few minutes and then transfer to a wire rack. Allow to cool fully before icing.

Topping

1 Meanwhile, combine all ingredients except the citrus zest and beat with an electric mixer for 5 minutes until creamy. Apply the topping to cupcakes. Sprinkle with mixed zests.

Makes 12 • Preparation 15 minutes • Cooking 25 minutes

Pink grapefruit cupcakes

2 eggs
125g (4.4oz) butter, softened
1 cup caster (berry) sugar
½ cup yoghurt
2 tablespoons grapefruit juice
zest of 1 pink grapefruit
2 cups self-raising flour, sifted
1 teaspoon vanilla extract

Topping
1½ cups icing sugar
125g (4.4oz) butter, softened
2 tablespoons pink grapefruit juice
1–2 drops pink colouring

1 Preheat the oven to 160°C (320°F). Line a 12-cupcake pan with cupcake papers. In a medium-sized bowl, lightly beat the eggs, add butter and sugar, then mix until light and fluffy.

2 Add yoghurt, grapefruit juice, grapefruit zest, flour and vanilla, and stir to combine. Beat with an electric mixer for 2 minutes, until light and creamy.

3 Divide the mixture evenly between the cake papers. Bake for 18–20 minutes until risen and firm to touch. Allow to cool for a few minutes and then transfer to a wire rack. Allow to cool fully before icing.

Topping
1 Meanwhile, combine half the icing sugar and butter, mix with a wooden spoon, add remaining sugar and butter and beat with the spoon until light and fluffy. Mix in pink grapefruit juice and colouring. Spread onto cupcakes.

Makes 12 • Preparation 12 minutes • Cooking 20 minutes

Weights and measures

Although recipes have been tested using the Australian Standard 250mL cup, 20mL tablespoon and 5mL teaspoon, they will work just as well with the US and Canadian 8 fl oz cup, or the UK 300mL cup. We have used graduated cup measures in preference to tablespoon measures so that proportions are always the same. Where tablespoon measures have been given, they are not crucial measures, so using the smaller tablespoon of the US or UK will not affect the recipe's success. But we all agree on the teaspoon size.

For breads, cakes and pastries, the only area which might cause concern is where eggs are used, as proportions will then vary. If working with a 250mL or 300mL cup, use large eggs (65g/2¼oz), adding a little more liquid to the recipe for 300mL cup measures if it seems necessary. Use medium-sized eggs (55g/2oz) with an 8 fl oz cup measure. A graduated set of measuring cups and spoons is recommended, the cups in particular for measuring dry ingredients. Remember to level such ingredients to ensure an accurate quantity.

Oven Temperatures
The Celsius temperatures given here are not exact; they have been rounded off and are given as a guide only. Follow the manufacturer's temperature guide, relating it to oven description given in the recipe. Remember gas ovens are hottest at the top, electric ovens at the bottom and convection-fan forced ovens are usually even throughout. We've included Regulo numbers for gas cookers, which may assist. To convert °C to °F multiply °C by 9 and divide by 5 then add 32.

	C°	F°	Gas Regulo
Very slow	120	250	1
Slow	150	300	2
Moderately slow	160	320	3
Moderate	180	350	4
Moderately hot	190–200	370–400	5–6
Hot	210–220	410–440	6–7
Very hot	230	450	8
Super hot	250–290	475–500	9–10

English Measures
English measurements are similar to Australian with two exceptions: the English cup measures 300mL/10½ fl oz, whereas the American and Australian cup measure 250mL/8¾ fl oz. The English tablespoon (the Australian dessertspoon) measures 14.8mL/½ fl oz against the Australian tablespoon of 20mL/¾ fl oz. The imperial measurement is 20 fl oz to the pint, 40 fl oz a quart and 160 fl oz per gallon.

American Measures
The American reputed pint is 16 fl oz, a quart is equal to 32 fl oz and the American gallon, 128 fl oz. The American tablespoon is equal to 14.8mL/½ fl oz, the teaspoon is 5mL/⅙ fl oz. The cup measure is 250mL/8¾ fl oz.

Dry Measures

All the measures are level, so when you have filled a cup or spoon, level it off with the edge of a knife. The scale below is the 'cook's equivalent'; it is not an exact conversion of metric to imperial measurement. To calculate the exact metric equivalent yourself, multiply ounces by 28.349523 to obtain grams, or divide grams by 28.349523 to obtain ounces.

Metric grams (g), kilograms (kg)	Imperial ounces (oz), pound (lb)	Metric grams (g), kilograms (kg)	Imperial ounces (oz), pound (lb)
15g	$\frac{1}{2}$oz	225g	8oz/$\frac{1}{2}$ lb
20g	$\frac{1}{3}$oz	315g	11oz
30g	1oz	340g	12oz/$\frac{3}{4}$ lb
55g	2oz	370g	13oz
85g	3oz	400g	14oz
115g	4oz/$\frac{1}{4}$ lb	425g	15oz
125g	4$\frac{1}{2}$oz	455g	16oz/1 lb
140/145g	5oz	1000g/1kg	35.3oz/2$\frac{1}{5}$ lb
170g	6oz	1$\frac{1}{2}$kg	3$\frac{1}{3}$ lb
200g	7oz		

Liquid Measures

Metric millilitres (mL)	Imperial fluid ounce (fl oz)	Cup and Spoon
5mL	$\frac{1}{6}$ fl oz	1 teaspoon
20mL	$\frac{2}{3}$ fl oz	1 tablespoon
30mL	1 fl oz	1 tbsp + 2 tsp
55mL	2 fl oz	
63mL	2$\frac{1}{4}$ fl oz	$\frac{1}{4}$ cup
85mL	3 fl oz	
115mL	4 fl oz	
125mL	4$\frac{1}{2}$ fl oz	$\frac{1}{2}$ cup
150mL	5$\frac{1}{4}$ fl oz	
188mL	6$\frac{2}{3}$ fl oz	$\frac{3}{4}$ cup
225mL	8 fl oz	
250mL	8 fl oz	1 cup
300mL	10$\frac{1}{2}$ fl oz	
370mL	13 fl oz	
400mL	14 fl oz	
438mL	15$\frac{1}{2}$ fl oz	1$\frac{3}{4}$ cups
455mL	16 fl oz	
500mL	17$\frac{1}{2}$ fl oz	2 cups
570mL	20 fl oz	
1 litre	35$\frac{1}{3}$ fl oz	4 cups

Index

Making a paper piping bag

1 Cut a 25cm (10in) square of greaseproof paper. Cut the square in half diagonally to form two triangles.

2 Place the paper triangles on top of each other and mark the three corners A, B and C.

3 Fold corner B around and inside corner A.

4 Bring corner C around the outside of the bag until it fits exactly behind corner A. At this stage all three corners should be together and the point closed.

5 Fold corner C over two or three times to hold the bag together. Snip the point off the bag and drop into an icing nozzle. The piping bag can also be used without a nozzle for writing and outlines, in which case only the very tip of the point should be snipped off.

Preparing a plastic bag for piping

We have included the basic explanation for how to prepare a piping bag. It is a handy skill if you have a piece of baking paper around, but if you find it a bit fiddly or if you don't have any paper on hand, the back-up trick is to fill the corner of a small plastic bag, simply roll it up and snip off the point. As long as the bag is sturdy enough and the person controlling the piping is gentle enough, the humble plastic bag can work wonderfully for applying line decorations or writing messages on individual cakes.

1

2

3